Changes In You
for Girls

by Peggy C. Siegel

Second Printing 1992, Third Printing 1994, Fourth Printing 1997

Published by
Family Life Education Associates
P.O. Box 7466
Richmond, Virginia 23221
(804) 262-0531

Library of Congress Catalog Card Number: 90-86237

ISBN 0-9628687-0-1

Printed in the United States of America

Book and cover design by Melissa Savage
and Sally Graybeal

Changes In You

A beautifully illustrated, simply worded explanation of the changes of puberty for girls

By Peggy C. Siegel
Illustrations by Vivien Cohen

Introduction

This book is about you. It is about how all girls change when they grow up. This is a very special time. But if you don't know about all these wonderful changes, they can be scary. This book was written to help you understand this exciting time in your life so that you can be happy and proud that you are growing up.

Some of the changes that you will go through, everyone can see and talk about. These changes are discussed in Part 1 of this book. Some changes are private. You should only talk about private changes with your parents, a teacher, a doctor or a best friend. Part 2, the private part of this book, begins on page 12.

Part 3 is about the new choices you may get to make as you are growing up.

Part 1

Public Changes

Each girl's body changes into a woman's body. Some girls start to change at age 9 or 10 and some when they are a little older, even at 16 years old. These girls are both 13 years old. One girl's body has grown and one has not. Some girls grow in a short amount of time. Some girls may take up to four years to make all the changes. This time of change is called puberty.

During puberty all girls grow taller and gain weight. But, they all grow at different times.

Not only do girls grow taller and gain weight, but their bodies change shape. Their hips get wider and their breasts grow. (Breasts are a private part of the body. They are talked about again on page 14.) Most girls like it when their hips and breasts begin to grow. They think it makes them look pretty and grown up.

Another change is that the body will smell differently
and the smell will be stronger. To keep the body smelling
nice, a girl needs to wash the underarm area and use a
deodorant every day. There are several types of deodorants
such as roll-ons and sticks. People talk about deodorant in
public, but everyone puts on their deodorant in a private
place like a bathroom or a bedroom.

Bad breath can also be a problem. Teens need to brush
and floss their teeth and use mouthwash every day. This
will keep a girl's teeth and gums healthy and her breath
smelling good.

A girl's skin also changes. The skin on the face becomes more oily. The changes in the skin make some girls get pimples (acne, zits). Pimples look like red sores on the face.

Teenagers need to keep their faces clean. It is important not to pick at or squeeze pimples. If pimples won't go away, a doctor can suggest soaps or medicine. He may also tell the teenager how important it is to eat good foods to help keep her skin healthy.

Another big change is that the hair on girls' arms and legs usually gets thicker. Hair also grows in the underarm area.

When girls become teenagers, some of them decide to shave off the hair on their legs and in their underarm area. There are two ways to shave. Shaving can be done with an electric razor like the teenager is doing in this picture. Also, if a teenager asks for help, she might be able to shave with shaving cream and a razor. Shaving is done in a private place like a bathroom.

During puberty, moods and feelings change too.
Sometimes girls get in sad moods. They feel like crying about everything or yelling at everyone. Girls also get in very happy moods. They feel silly and can't stop giggling. Other times they may get so excited that they feel like they can't calm down.

It is important to remember that it is normal to have these strong moods and feelings.

Girls do different things to help themselves get over sad moods. Usually it helps a girl to talk about her feelings with someone who understands. Some girls find that it helps to walk or exercise. Sitting with a friend can make the sad feelings go away too. And sometimes, just being alone is a good idea.

If a girl has sad feelings that never seem to go away she may need to ask for help. Parents or teachers can find a counselor who can help her.

Part 2

Private Changes

This part of the book is private. You can look at it alone or read it and talk about it with a parent, teacher, doctor or a best friend. It should only be read and looked at in a private place like a bedroom or some other place where you can be alone.

In this section of the book there are some new, important words to learn. You may have learned some different words, but this part of the book uses the words doctors and most adults use when they are talking about the body and how it works.

There are three parts of a girl's body that are private. The breasts (boobs, tits), the vulva (pubic area) and the buttocks (bottom, rear end). Girls and women keep the breasts, vulva and buttocks covered when they are in public because these body parts are special and private.

During puberty, one of the first changes in a girl's body is that her breasts grow. This is a wonderful sign that soon she will have the body of a woman.

As a girl's breasts grow, they may feel sore. It is normal for breasts to be sensitive during this time.

Some girls worry because they think that their breasts are too small or too big. This drawing shows that women have breasts and nipples which are different sizes and shapes. All women have breasts that are attractive and a beautiful part of their bodies.

When a girl's breasts begin to grow, she will probably need to buy a bra. Bras are bought in the ladies' underwear section of a department store. There are many different kinds of bras. A girl needs to try on different ones to see which kind fits her best.

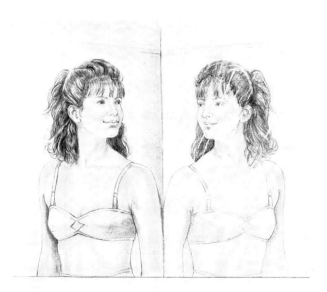

This girl has found a bra that is just right for her. It feels good and will make her clothes look nice.

Another private change that a girl can see during puberty is that pubic hair grows between her legs and on and around the vulva. Pubic hair is the name for this curly hair.

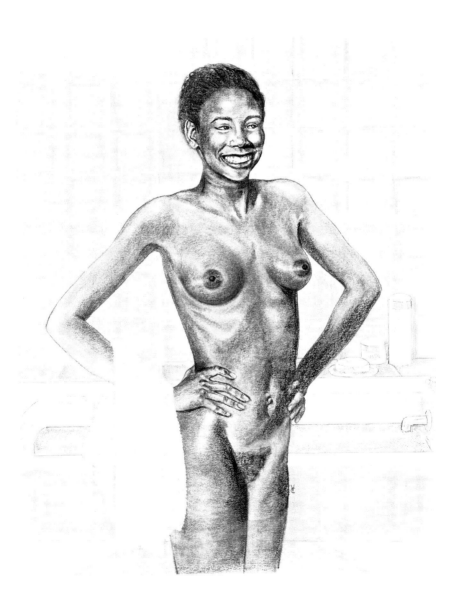

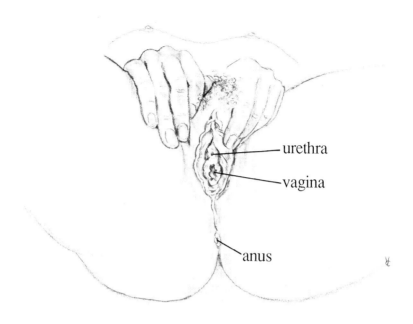

urethra

vagina

anus

The biggest change that happens during puberty is that girls begin to menstruate or have a period once a month. But before periods are explained, girls need to know a few more things about how their bodies work.

This is a drawing of a woman's vulva area (private parts) when she is lying down and her legs are spread apart.

Girls and women have three holes between their legs: the urethra is in the front, the vagina is in the middle and the anus is in the back. Each of these holes has a special job to do. It is important to know how the eating and drinking systems of the body work because the urethra and the anus are part of these systems.

This is how the drinking system works. When a person drinks a liquid, like juice, it goes into the mouth and down the throat. Then it goes down the food pipe and into the stomach. When the liquid leaves the stomach, it goes to the kidneys where the body takes out all the vitamins it needs. After the body takes what it needs, the rest of the liquid goes down to the bladder. The bladder keeps all the liquid that the body doesn't need. When the bladder is full, a girl feels like she has to go to the bathroom. When a girl goes to the bathroom, liquid that's called urine (water, pee) goes out of the bladder and comes out of the hole between her legs called the urethra (pee hole).

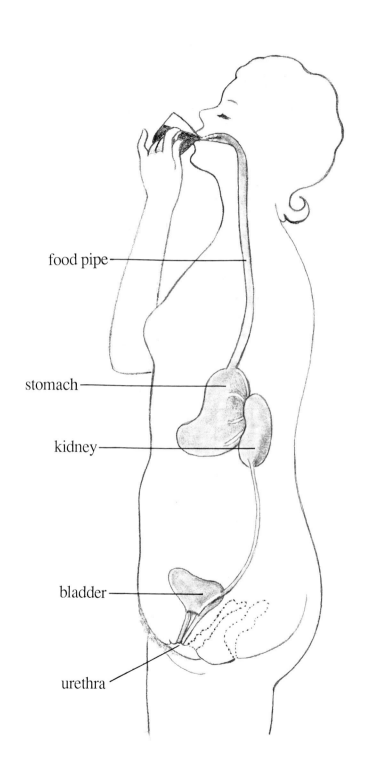

food pipe

stomach

kidney

bladder

urethra

The eating system works like this. When a person eats food it goes into the mouth, where she chews it. Then it goes down the food pipe into the stomach. When the food leaves the stomach, it goes into the intestines, so that the body can take out all the vitamins and minerals it needs. The rest of the food is waste (like trash) and must be removed from the body. This waste is called a bowel movement or BM (poop, crap). The BM goes out of the anus which is the hole between the buttocks (butt, rear end).

BMs have a strong odor. It is important to wipe the buttocks carefully to stay clean and smelling nice.

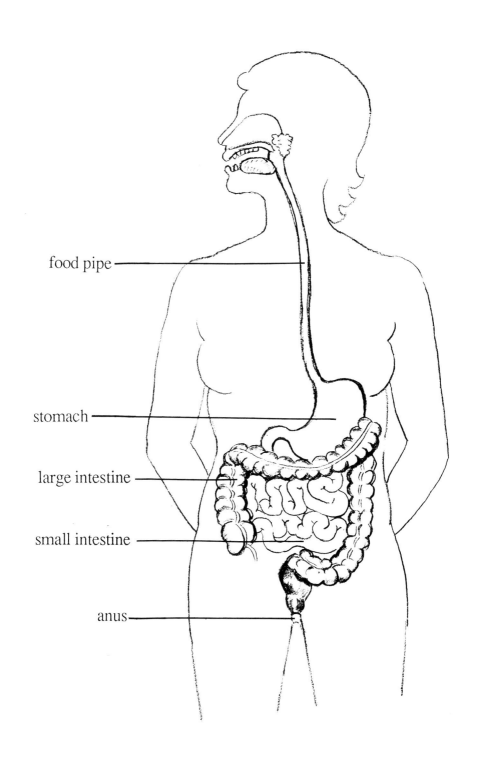

food pipe

stomach

large intestine

small intestine

anus

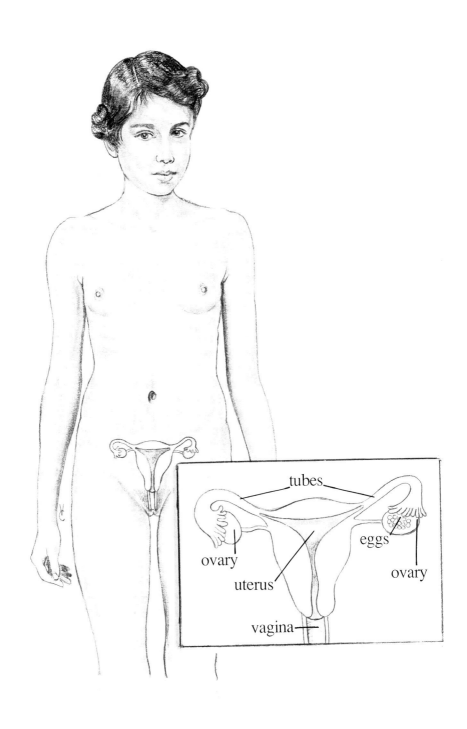

tubes

ovary

eggs

uterus

ovary

vagina

The vagina is the other hole between the legs. It is the opening to some special parts inside the body that only girls and women have. This is a drawing of these special parts. The ovaries (egg sacs) hold tiny, tiny eggs and the tube connects the ovaries to the uterus (womb). It takes one of these tiny eggs from a woman's ovaries (egg sacs) and a sperm from a man to make a baby. The uterus (womb) is the place where a baby grows when a woman is pregnant.

When a girl reaches puberty, one egg comes out of the ovary (egg sac) each month. Each egg is as small as this dot (·). It comes down one of the tubes and into the uterus (womb). This is a very special time. Girls can't see or feel the egg moving down the tube into the uterus.

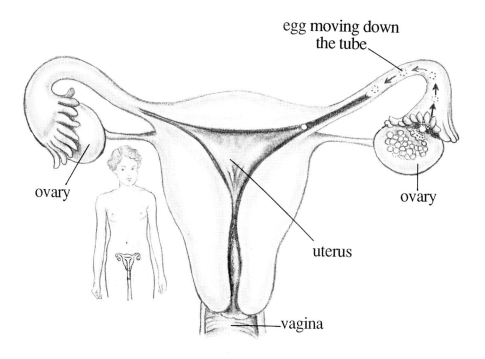

egg moving down the tube

ovary

ovary

uterus

vagina

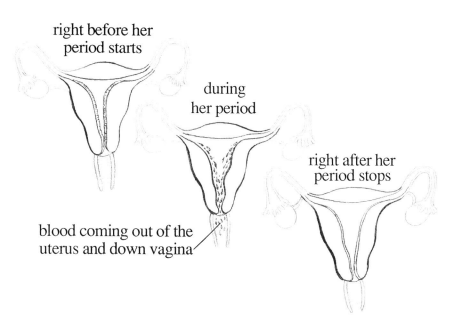

right before her
period starts

during
her period

right after her
period stops

blood coming out of the
uterus and down vagina

At the same time the egg is coming down the tube, the inside of the uterus is getting thicker with blood. After about two weeks, the blood and the egg come out. The blood comes down and out the vagina. The egg comes out too, but it is too small to see. When the blood comes out the vagina this is called menstruation or having a period.

Menstruation, or having a period, happens to all girls. It is normal and healthy. Most girls have their first period when they are between 11 and 13 years old. Some girls start their periods when they are younger or older. Once a girl starts her period, she will have it about once a month. Each month her period will last for about 4 or 5 days and nights.

Girls and women need to take care of themselves in special ways when they have their period. Girls need to use a pad (sanitary napkin) or a tampon to absorb (catch) the blood that is coming out of the vagina. Pads or tampons need to be worn during the day and at night when a girl has her period.

This picture shows some different types of pads. Most girls use pads that have a sticky strip on the bottom so they can be attached to underpants easily.

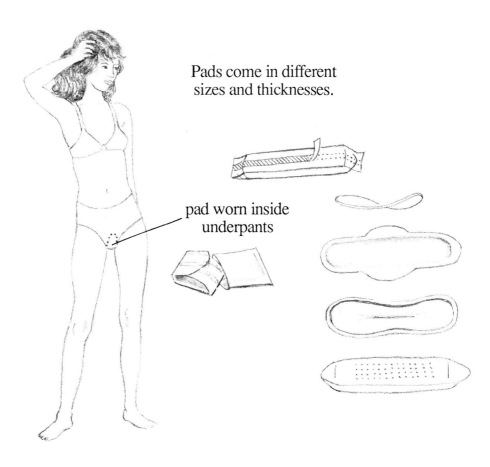

Pads come in different sizes and thicknesses.

pad worn inside underpants

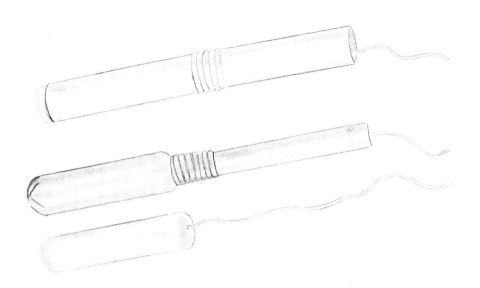

These are tampons. Tampons are long pieces of cotton that some girls put in their vagina to absorb (catch) the blood before it comes out of their body.

These pictures show how the tampon is put into the vagina.

This girl is thinking about what it will be like to start her period. She knows that there are many different types of pads and tampons. She should try several to see which kind she likes best. Pads and tampons can be bought at a drug store, grocery store or department store.

DISPOSAL

A girl needs to change her pad or tampon every few hours when she has her period. This is done in the bathroom in private. First, if a girl uses a pad, she wraps the used pad in toilet paper. Then she throws it in the bathroom trash can. She never puts the used pad in the toilet. It can clog up the toilet. A tampon needs to be changed every few hours too. Tampons can usually be flushed down the toilet. They can also be wrapped and thrown away just like a pad.

After a girl takes off the used pad or tampon, she needs to put on a new one until, of course, her period stops.

A girl should try to remember to carry a pad or tampon in her purse in case she needs it. If a girl starts her period and she does not have a pad or tampon with her, she can buy one from a machine in the women's restroom.

It is helpful for a girl to learn when to expect her next period. Remember, girls get their periods about every four weeks or once a month. It is a good idea for a girl to mark off the days on her calendar that she has her period. This way she will know when her next period should start. If this is hard to figure out, her mother, teacher or nurse can help her mark her calendar.

It is very important for girls to wash between the folds of skin of the vulva area. When a girl has her period she needs to wash even more carefully around the vulva when she is taking her shower or bath.

Sometimes when a girl has her period she gets cramps. Cramps can feel very uncomfortable, like a low, tight stomachache. If a girl has bad cramps, she should talk to her mother or the school nurse, or go see a doctor. They can suggest things to do that will help her feel better.

During their periods, some girls feel a little tired or sad for a day or two. Most girls feel fine during their periods. They go to school, take P.E., exercise, do chores, dance or whatever they usually do.

Another thing that changes during puberty is that a girl may start having new private feelings. She may think about boys more and have sexy thoughts. When a girl feels sexy, she may touch her private body parts (breasts or vulva area). This is called masturbation (playing with yourself). Some girls do not like to touch their private body parts.

Remember, the breasts and vulva area are private, so touching them is a very private thing to do. If a girl wants to do this, she should be alone in a private place like the bathroom or her bedroom with the door closed.

Part 3

Life Changes — Making Choices

One of the wonderful changes that happens when you grow up is that you get to start making more choices. This part of the book is about making choices that will help you be safe, healthy and happy.

If you learn to make choices that keep you safe and healthy, then people who love you will be so proud of you. They will want you to make other new choices for yourself. If you make choices that are dangerous or make you sick, they will worry about you. They will want to protect you, so instead of you making choices for yourself, they will make choices for you.

As you grow up, try to show the people you love that you can make good choices about how to act and how to take care of yourself.

Making good choices is an exciting part of growing up.

One of the biggest choices a girl has is how to take care of her body. As a girl grows she will have more choices about what kind of snacks and meals she would like. One good way to take care of the body is to choose to eat good foods, like the ones in this picture. Good food helps the bones grow, muscles get stronger and the skin to look nice. It helps a girl stay healthy. Junk food like soft drinks, chips and sweets do not help the body grow or stay healthy.

Another way a girl can choose to take care of her body is to exercise. Regular exercise helps girls to grow up strong and healthy. Some girls walk, ride bikes, swim or do aerobics to make sure they get enough exercise. This helps girls feel better about how they look.

Girls can also take care of themselves by choosing to get enough sleep. This helps girls stay healthy and happy. If a girl decides to stay up late watching TV every night, she will be too tired to have fun during the day. Staying up late might make her feel grouchy and upset. Her friends and family will not like her acting this way. A girl can choose to help her body grow and stay healthy by getting enough sleep. Sleep can help her feel happier about her life too!

One of the biggest choices a girl has now is deciding how she wants to look. If she wants other people to like being with her, she needs to do things that will help her look clean and neat, and will help keep her smelling nice. She needs to decide to take a shower or bath every day. She needs to take special care in washing the underarm area and between the legs. Then it is important for her to remember to put on deodorant every morning. She will also look great if she washes her face, hair and nails carefully.

It is OK for a girl to ask for help or advice. The important thing is that a girl makes the choice to look nice.

It is a grown-up responsibility to learn to take care of the body. Parents are very proud of their daughters when they see them making good decisions about how to take care of their bodies.

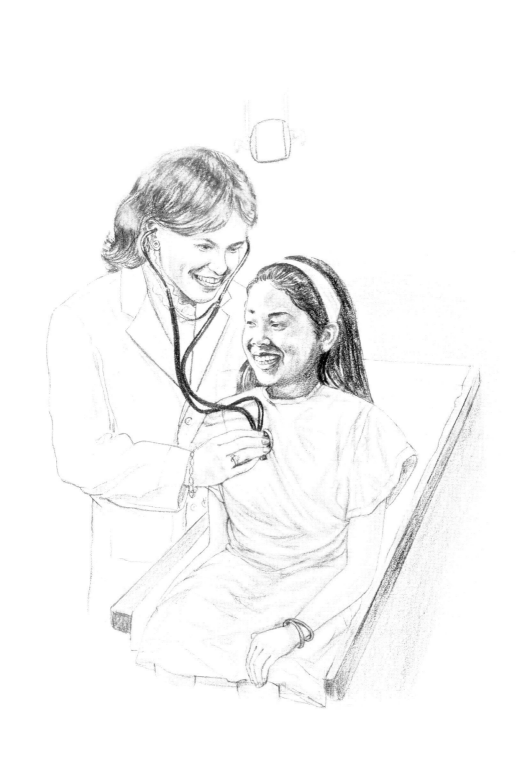

Another way girls can take care of their health is by going to the doctor for a check-up once a year. The doctor checks the eyes, ears, throat, heart and lungs. She/he also looks at the private body parts. The doctor looks at the breasts and then between the legs to check the urethra, vagina and anus.

Once a girl's body changes, she may go to a special woman's doctor called a gynecologist. This doctor does a breast examination and a pelvic examination. In the breast examination she/he checks a woman's breasts to make sure she does not have any problems. The pelvic examination is to make sure the special inside parts of her body are healthy. The doctor checks the vagina, uterus (womb) and ovaries (egg sacs). This kind of check-up can seem scary if a girl is not prepared. A girl should ask her mom or a nurse to tell her more about pelvic examinations and breast examinations before she has this kind of check-up.

When the doctor gives a girl a check-up, he usually finds that she is healthy and that everything is fine.

Sometimes in between check-ups a girl may have a problem with her private body parts. She needs to see a doctor if:

1. Her period is very, very heavy, she stops having her period or if she bleeds between periods.
2. Her cramps are so bad that she has to stay in bed.
3. She finds a lump in her breast.
4. She feels pain or a burning feeling when she goes to the bathroom.
5. She sees blood in the urine or BM.
6. She has any sores on her vulva area.
7. Her vagina or vulva area itches, burns or feels sore.
8. She has a discharge (unusual white or yellow liquid) from her vagina that looks or smells different.

Sometimes it is hard to talk about private problems. But it is a good choice for a girl to tell her parents so they can call a doctor if she has any of these problems. Doctors know how to help girls who are having problems with their private body parts.

If a girl wants to show others that she is growing up, it is important for her to know how to act in public.

———————————

There are some laws about private body parts that most girls already know about and that are important to remember.

1. The breasts, vulva and buttocks are special and private. Girls and women do not show their private body parts in public.
2. Masturbation (touching private body parts) is private. Girls and women need to remember not to touch their private body parts when they are in a public place.

There are some other important laws that help protect girls and women. One important law to know about is:

No one is allowed to touch a girl's private body parts unless she wants to be touched.

It is so important for a girl to learn to appreciate that her body is beautiful and special. It is something that belongs to her.

If someone tries to touch a girl's private body parts and she doesn't want them to, she needs to decide to protect herself. She can do this by looking straight at the person and saying "NO" loudly in a mean voice. Then she should try to get away.

When someone tries to or does touch a girl's private body parts, the girl needs to decide to tell her parents, a teacher or another adult she trusts. If they do not believe her, she should tell someone else until someone does believe her.

It is the right choice to tell someone. They will not be angry with her. They will know it's not her fault. They will want what is safe and good for her. And they will try to help her.

In this part of the book you have been told about many different choices you can make. Some of these choices are very hard to make. It is hard to choose foods that are good for you when you think some junk foods taste better. It may be hard to choose to talk to parents or the doctor about problems with private body parts. It may be hard to choose to protect yourself. But these hard choices will help you be healthy, happy and safe. And they will make you feel proud that you are able to make good choices.

After reading this book, you may have questions. Please ask an adult who you trust, like a parent, a teacher or a doctor, to help you understand all these changes.

Changing from being a girl to a woman is a very exciting time in your life. Your body is growing in so many beautiful ways. Your feelings are changing. And you have new exciting choices to make. You can feel proud and happy about all these wonderful changes.